What's So Great About King Tut?
A Biography of Tutankhamun Just for Kids!
Max Tanner

KidLit-O Books
www.kidlito.com

© 2014. All Rights Reserved.

Cover Image © Christopher Dodge - Fotolia.com

Table of Contents

About KidCaps

KidLit-O is an imprint of BookCaps™ that is just for kids! Each month BookCaps will be releasing several books in this exciting imprint. Visit are website or like us on Facebook to see more!

To add your name to our mailing list, visit this link: http://www.kidlito.com/mailing-list.html

The burial mask worn by King Tut[1]

[1]   Image:
http://commons.wikimedia.org/wiki/File:King_Tut_Ankh_Amun_G
olden_Mask.jpg

Chapter 1: Introduction

The young boy furrowed his brow as he carefully studied the board. He needed to move his last piece off of the board to win the game, but the only way to do so would be to move it six spaces during his next turn. A six was the most difficult number to throw, and young Tutankhaten wasn't having the best of luck today.

Taking a deep breath, Tutankhaten grabbed the marked sticks, rubbed them between his hands, and threw them down onto the table. All four sticks landed with their marked sides up, which meant that he could move his piece the six spaces he needed to! With a youthful giggle Tutankhaten moved his piece off of the board and put it together with the others.

Looking looked up at his father, Pharaoh Amenhotep IV, Tutankhaten smiled. The young prince had won this round fair and square, and his father the Egyptian King was happy to see his young son using his sharp mind to develop strategies and to calculate odds.

"Do you want to play again, father?" Tutankhaten asked. Pharaoh Amenhotep IV shook his head. "I am afraid that I cannot, my son. I have many duties to attend to, and I must visit the priests of Aten to answer some questions they have for me. In fact, perhaps you could come along and work a little with your father? It would be good for you to see what the life of a Pharaoh is like. After all, you too will sit in the throne after I journey to the next world. It is the gift that our family gives to Egypt."

Although Tutankhaten knew that one day he would have to do the same work his father now did, he wasn't too excited about it. He preferred to play games, practice his archery, and to learn about military tactics. His wet-nurse Maia used to entertain him with stories about princesses and princes, but since she stopped taking care of him, Tut no longer heard many fairy tales.

Tut's father Amenhotep gave him a blessing and then left Tut alone with a guard. The boy lifted himself to his feet with some difficulty and grabbed his little cane so he could hobble over towards the door and out into the courtyard. As he sat down on a small seat, he could hear many Egyptians outside of the courtyard walls as they went about their daily business. Some were buying and selling; others were sitting and making beautiful garments of bright white linen; and still others were walking down the Royal Road towards the Great Temple, where they would go to consult with the priests of the sun-disk god Aten.

Tut lived in the capital city of Akhetaten (Amarna)[2]

Living in the city that his father had built, Tutankhaten felt a real sense of pride. While he couldn't understand all of the reasons why his father had moved the Egyptian capital city from Thebes to Akhetaten, he knew that his father was happy with the decision and that most of the people of this city respected the king. The priests bowed whenever they saw Amenhotep IV or Tutankhaten, and the people around him seemed to have plenty of food to eat and work to do.

Tutankhaten liked living here in the royal palace. Even though his left foot hurt when he walked and his health didn't let him do all of the things other little boys did, eight-year old Tut knew that he was born into a special family. More than that, Tut knew that a lot of people thought that he was a pretty special kid.

[2] Image source: http://nl.defaraosenhunkoninginnen.wikia.com/wiki/Akhetaten/Tel-el_Amarna

For now, Tut spent his days playing games and taking classes, learning how to read and write and about army strategies and weapons. But the day would soon come when Tut would no longer have time for fun and games, a time when he would have to put into practice all of the military tactics that he had learned.

Tut could hardly have known that his life would drastically change in just a couple of years. His father Amenhotep IV would die and Tut would sit down on a throne as the King of all Egypt. Tutankhaten could also hardly imagine that more than 3,000 years later, the entire world would know who he was, how he had lived his life, and that they would affectionately call him "The Boy Pharaoh".

Born as "Tutankhaten" (and later changing his name to "Tutankhamen" or "Tutankhamun"), this remarkable young man is remembered for many reasons. During his reign as Pharaoh he made the difficult decision to publically disagree with his father and to undo many of the changes that Amenhotep IV had made during his rule (including making Amarna the capital city). Tutankhaten would also try to reestablish the friendships with surrounding nations that his father had ignored and to start a large family of his own so that his ideas could continue to guide the country long after he had died.

But the life of Tutankhaten was very complicated. It seems that as a young king he was used by the people around him, specifically some very powerful advisors who took advantage of the fact that he was just a child. They probably convinced the king to do the things that they themselves wanted him to do.

After his death and burial, Tut's tomb was hidden away for over 3,000 years before finally being discovered in 1922. When his tomb was opened to the world, King Tutankhaten was once again used by the people surrounding him – this time by archeologists and Egyptologists trying to understand the world that Tut had grown up in. The personal possessions that Tut had been buried with were separated and shipped from one museum to another, and people around the world read about his life and death as if they were reading a novel.

So many words have been written about King Tutankhaten, but the fact is that very few people know the real story of who this young king was and what kinds of things he did. Far from being just "a boy Pharaoh", Tutankhaten was alive during a time of radical change in Egypt, and he had the incredible responsibility to guide his beloved nation down the right path and to try and make decisions that would benefit all of his countrymen.

Not only did Tut have to protect his people from being taken advantage of by nearby nations, he also had to protect them from corrupt politicians and priests within his borders. Tut was also expected to be the religious leader of the land, deciding how all Egyptians should worship and how much religious freedom they should have.

Much of what we know about Ancient Egypt comes from the tombs of pharaohs like Tut and the possessions, construction projects, and writings that each generation left behind. That is one of the reasons why King Tut and his life are so important. Because nobody went into his tomb for such a long time, archaeologists have been able to learn a lot about what life was like for people who were living way back then, including what kinds of things were important not only to the average Egyptian, but also for King Tut in particular.

This very special boy Pharaoh came from a long line of royalty. But just because he had important parents didn't mean that Tut had an easy life, free of problems. In fact, being born in the spotlight brought him all sorts of special difficulties.

Tut had to deal with bad health from the time that he was young, and he would go on to experience one tragedy after another in his personal life, including two children who died before they could be born. Tut likely felt manipulated by the people around him and sometimes wondered who really was on his side. And as he went to sleep each night, Tut probably asked himself whether or not the decisions that he had made that day were really in the best interests of his people.

It's never easy to be the one in charge.

The story of King Tut really began with his father, King Amenhotep IV, and the changes that this unpopular pharaoh made in the land of Ancient Egypt.

Chapter 2: The Early Life and Education of King Tut

Amenhotep IV ruled Egypt for about 17 years during a time known as the 18th dynasty of Egypt. A "dynasty" is a series of rulers who all have the same origin, usually a specific family. During the 18th dynasty of Egypt, each king was somehow related to the previous king, either through blood or some other close relationship.

The 18th dynasty included fifteen pharaohs who ruled for some 250 years. Some of them ruled for decades while others only ruled for one or two years.

During his time on the throne, Amenhotep IV made some big changes in the way that average Egyptians lived their lives. He changed the way they worshipped, the way they interacted with other nations, and he even changed where the king and his family lived.

As Amenhotep IV (who later changed his name to "Akhenaten") made one unpopular change after another, some people in Egypt started to feel unhappy with what the king was doing. They wanted life to go back to the way that it had been before.

What kinds of changes did Amenhotep IV make that were so unpopular? Here's an example.

For a long time, people in Egypt had practiced something called "a *polytheistic* religion". A polytheistic religion is one that worships many gods, often believing that each one has a special job to do, and that no gods should be ignored.

But Amenhotep IV thought that the god *Aten* (who was represented by the disk of the sun) was the most important god and that it should receive more attention than the rest. If fact, Amenhotep IV felt so strongly about worshipping Aten that he changed his name to "Akhenaten" – which meant "Effective for Aten". In other words, the king was making it known that from that point on his life would revolve only around the worship of Aten.

But changing his name to draw more attention to Aten wasn't enough for the king. He still thought that others were talking too much about other gods – those gods that Egyptians had been worshipping for centuries.

Akhenaten used his power as king to change the laws of Egypt and to make it illegal to worship any god but Aten. That law not only affected the lives of the people who had previously worshipped other gods (like Horus, Osiris, and Isis), it also took away the power and money of the other gods' priests.

Back in Egypt, a priest was more than just a religious teacher; each one also played an important role in serving the people and in helping the government to function. For example, some priests determined boundary lines; others collected taxes; and still others were doctors and took care of preparing dead bodies for burial.

But Akhenaten wasn't done yet. He had greater ideas of how Egypt should be organized.

He decided to move the capital city from Thebes to a new city that he personally had built. He called the city Akhetaten – which meant "Horizon of Aten" (although today most archeologists call the city "Amarna").

When one of his wives got pregnant and gave birth to a son about the year 1341 BC, Akhenaten continued with his religious zeal and named the boy Tutankhaten – which meant "The image of Aten". While Akhenaten's queen was named Nefertiti (who went on to become a famous queen and maybe even a Pharaoh herself), it was one of the king's other wives (most likely his full sister) who was the mother of Tutankhaten.

For Akhenaten, nothing was as important for the king than to promote the religion of Aten. All of his other duties, which included things like keeping good relations with nearby nations, were ignored as Akhenaten focused on making his favorite god more and more important in Egypt.

It's not hard to understand why some people were unhappy with the changes that Akhenaten made. In the span of just a few short years, Akhenaten had managed to change everything about Egyptian culture and daily life. The laws he made and the policies he enforced put some people out of jobs, made others feel their opinions didn't matter, and caused Egypt to stop being friends with countries that had helped them over the years.

Although Akhenaten was popular with some people (especially those who got the power that previously belonged to the priests), he had started to make some very powerful enemies, including priestly families and members of the military.

But apart from what he did as king, some people were shocked by the choices that Akhenaten made in his personal life. For example, it may seem strange for us today to read about two close family members who get married and have kids, but the fact is that in different parts of the world, that is simply the way many kings and queens lived their lives. Every time a prince or princess got married, there was a chance that the family might lose some of their power.

So one method that some royal families used (including the Habsburgs of Europe) was to only allow young princes and princesses to marry close family members, thus preventing other families from stealing away their political power.

Unfortunately, any children born into a marriage of close relatives will almost always have some problems, due to complications with DNA. For example, one parent may have a small problem in their DNA that would normally be hidden by the DNA of the other parent. That is why most children are born healthy and without any major illnesses, even though each parent's DNA may have a few problems here and there.

But when two close family members have a baby together, it is very likely that each parent's DNA has the same errors in the same places. When this happens, problems that might otherwise have been cancelled out are instead magnified, and the child is born with sickness and deformities.

That is what happened to young Tutankhaten. From the moment that he was born, it was probably clear that little Tutankhaten was going to be a sick child. His left foot was twisted in and shaped strangely, his spine was slightly curved, his head sloped backwards into a cone, and his mouth had a hole in its roof called a cleft palate. Unfortunately, most of Tut's family members had similar health problems.

But Tut's disabilities, while severe, probably didn't prevent him from enjoying many of the activities that other little boys and girls enjoyed, including playing board games. But Tut would always be aware that he was different. It's not just that he had to live apart from the other little girls and boys his age, or that he had to spend time learning how to shoot a bow and arrow and how to wear armor in battle.

No, it was hard for the young prince to forget about his health problems because of the trouble that he had with even simple tasks like standing and walking. From a very young age, young King Tut needed a cane to walk. When his tomb was opened thousands of years later, there were about 130 canes buried inside with him, many showing heavy usage.

Growing up in the palace at Akhetaten (Amarna) was very exciting, and young Tut got to see people coming in from all around the kingdom, people who wanted to see his father and to conduct business in the capital. He would have had a busy life in the palace for sure, but there would have also been time for games.

Tut loved games. How do we know?

Because Egyptians believed that a person could take personal objects with them into the afterlife, they often placed a person's cherished toys, pets, and even servants into their tomb with their body. So what kinds of things were found in Tut's tomb that can show us the things that were important to him as a child?

More than anything, archaeologists were surprised to see four board games that had been buried with the young king. It seems that Tut spent many long hours as a child playing games of strategy and chance. One of them – described in the introduction – was called "Senet". Each player had to throw several sticks, and depending on how the sticks landed, they could move their pieces forward a certain number of spaces. The goal was to be the first to move all of the pieces off the board.

One of the games of Senet that was buried with King Tut[3]

But while life in the palace meant meeting important people and always having the best of everything, there were surely difficult moments for Tut. Although he probably never fought in any wars because of his poor health, he did have to face a different sort of battle every day: dealing with constant illness (including several bouts of malaria transmitted through mosquito bites).

[3] Image: http://www.touregypt.net/museum/tutI69.htm

He also had to accept the fact that most of his life's important decisions had already been made for him.

Tut couldn't decide what job he wanted to do; he was destined to be a Pharaoh. He couldn't decide who he would marry; his half-sister Ankhesenpaaten had already been chosen for him. He couldn't even decide how to spend his time because he was constantly being trained for the day when he would be king.

And though we can't be sure, it is likely that Tut had at least some idea that his father had made some unpopular choices as king. Tut likely knew that the priests who had previously helped the people to worship other gods wanted their temples back. He probably also knew that other countries (like Syria) felt that Egypt wasn't being nice to them anymore, even though Syria had helped Egypt in the past.

And in a time where people blamed gods and kings for everything, a fast-moving disease (likely influenza or the plague) that had passed through the land of Egypt during the reign of Akhenaten probably made some people think that the king of Egypt and his new laws were angering the gods.

It was in this environment that Tut was born and was raised. He was surrounded by powerful people, some of whom who supported his father and others who didn't. Tut saw how much his father's Egyptian subjects wanted a different life from the one they had, and Tut probably couldn't help but wonder what he would be able to do to make his people happier when it was finally his turn to be king.

But there was another difficulty. Even if Tut accepted his fate to one day be Pharaoh of Egypt, he couldn't really choose when he wanted to start the new job. Tut knew that the only way that he would ever get to sit on the throne would be if his father Akhenaten died.

Young Tut likely had mixed emotions as he grew up. He loved his father but may not have agreed with the changes that he had made. He may not have wanted to marry his half-sister, but he felt a certain responsibility to keep his family's reputation strong and to help them stay in power. He may not have wanted to be king – especially if it meant benefitting from his father's death – but at the same time he *did* desperately want the people of Egypt to have happy lives and he knew that only if he were king could he truly help them.

So when Akhenaten finally died when Tut was about 9 or 10 years old, it probably felt kind of strange for the boy. On one hand, Tut missed his father terribly and may not have felt ready to be king; but on the other hand, he knew that the time had come for Tut to do some good for the people of Egypt. For about a year after Akhenaten died, it seems that another person (possibly Akhenaten's Queen Nefertiti) ruled the land for a year or so, but soon it was time for Tut to fulfill his destiny.

And so at just ten years old or so, Tutankhaten - son of Amenhotep IV - became king of one of the most powerful nations in history.

Chapter 3: The Career of King Tut

It couldn't have been easy to become king at such a young age. While most kids worried about playing with their friends or learning a new trade from their parents, Tut had to worry about leading a nation and fighting wars. He had to learn to look for guidance from above, how to stop rebellions, and how to keep Egypt's national economy strong and healthy. He also had to learn how to identify traitors and how to protect his position as king.

As soon as he became pharaoh, Tut celebrated his wedding to his bride Ankhesenpaaten (his half-sister and daughter of Queen Nefertiti), who was just a few years older than he was. Tut was about 10 years old and Ankhesenpaaten was probably around 13. As soon as they were old enough, the two children would try to start a family of their own and to have as many kids as they could (though as we will see, this didn't happen). Tut would be expected to continue the family dynasty that had been ruling over Egypt for more than 200 years.

Becoming king while still a child was very difficult, but Tut wasn't left to do the job by himself; he had the help of a team of advisors that included two very experienced men. The men who offered to help Tut run the country were an Army General named Horemheb and a Grand Vizier (Prime Minister) named Ay. Both Horemheb and Ay had served their country when Tut's father Akhenaten was Pharaoh, and both would continue to do so now that Tut was king.

But because Tut was so young, it soon became clear that Horemheb and Ay were the power behind Tut's throne. They were the ones in charge and it was them who decided most of what Tut would do and when he would do it.

Ay (who was actually Tut's great uncle) had been a soldier in the military before serving as a powerful advisor to Tut's father Akhenaten (and possibly even to Tut's grandfather Amenhotep III). He was born into a noble family as the son of a priest, and archeologists have found some evidence that makes them think Ay may have been the father-in-law of one of two Pharaohs: either of Amenhotep III or of Akhenaten (which means that he was the father either of Amenhotep III's queen Tiye or of Akhenaten's queen Nefertiti).

In his position as Prime Minister and advisor to the King of Egypt, Ay helped Tut to make some very important decisions and to care for many of the day-to-day affairs of the kingdom. His long patience during the reign of Akhenaten had finally paid off.

Ay's father had been a priest, yet Ay kept his mouth shut and went along with King Akhenaten and his efforts to focus all worship on the sun god Aten. And although he may not personally have agreed with all that Akhenaten was doing, Ay recognized that his job was to provide advice. He knew that at the end of the day, only the Pharaoh's opinion mattered

It is also likely that at least one of Ay's parents was not from Egypt (his father was probably from Syria to the northeast), and this heritage may have caused mixed feelings as Ay watched Akhenaten ignore Egypt's allies in Syria and focus solely on religious goals at home.

When young Tut became king in place of his father, Ay saw an opportunity to undo the changes that Akhenaten had made – changes that (in Ay's opinion) had been bad for Egypt. For 25 years, Ay had watched his beloved Egypt be ruled by a family that he didn't always agree with, and now all that would change.

Prime Minister Ay was an advisor to King Tut[4]

General Horemheb, too, had mixed feelings about the changes that Akhenaten had made as pharaoh. In the beginning of his political career, Horemheb worked for the king as a travelling representative of Egypt. Part of his job description was visiting the governors of the nearby nation of Nubia and receiving visitors from other countries (including the Prince of Miam). Horemheb was not born into an important priestly family as Ay had been – his was a common family - but it seems that Horemheb's

[4] Image: http://en.wikipedia.org/wiki/Ay

talents and political mind had helped him to gain the attention of the king and the royal court.

Put simply, Horemheb believed in government and politics. He thought that the best way to solve a nation's problems was people putting their minds together. Like most Egyptians, Horemheb was probably at least a little religious and he surely respected the rights of others to worship as they wanted - but ultimately he believed that a well-organized government should run the country. He didn't think that priests should have all the power – at least not priests that Horemheb didn't personally know and trust.

When Tut's father Akhenaten took power from the priests of Amen (also known as "Amun") and gave their political power to his friends (even moving the capital city to Amarna), Horemheb was not happy. In his opinion, changing so much about the culture and organization of the nation was making outside nations lose their respect for Egypt. Horemheb felt that the land that he loved was losing its reputation as a stable and strong country.

It felt like everything was in chaos.

So when young Tut became King of Egypt, Ay wasn't the only one who thought that he could take advantage of the "Boy Pharaoh" - Horemheb also thought that he might be able to correct some of the wrongs that he felt Akhenaten had done. But unlike Ay – who wanted to give all the power back to the priests of Amen – Horemheb wanted to give power mainly to politicians and judges. He might give some power back to the priests, but only if he could be sure that those priests wouldn't let the power go to their heads.

Horemheb had strong opinions about how power should be divided in Egypt[5]

---

[5] Image: http://en.wikipedia.org/wiki/Horemheb

It's not hard to imagine that at times young Tut felt like he was being pulled in all directions at once by his group of advisors, especially by Ay and Horemheb. After all, Tut was just a kid who no doubt wanted to be a good king but who couldn't really be expected to understand the complex politics and opinions of the people around him. Because he was so young, it seems like Tut ended up just doing the things that Ay, Horemheb, and his other advisors wanted him to do.

For example, one of Tut's first actions as Pharaoh was to bring Egypt back to a *polytheistic* culture – completely the opposite of what his father had done. While his father Akhenaten had tried to make all Egyptians worship just one god (the sun-disk god Aten) Tut let people worship as many gods as they wanted.

Tut took these reforms very personally. To show how committed he was to the people's god Amen (and to show how different he was from his father), Tut decided to change his name from Tutankhaten ("Living image of Aten") to Tutankhamen ("Living image of Amen").

This was a very important move – both religiously and politically. It would be like a President who had been named after a Christian Saint (like "Peter" or "Paul") beginning to call himself by an Islamic name (like "Abdul Maalik", which means "Slave of the Lord").

While some people might not be happy with a change like that, if there were enough people in his country that supported his new religion, then the name change would make him very popular. And that is exactly what happened with Tut.

After Tut changed his name to Tutankhamen, his half-sister and wife (the daughter of Akhenaten and Nefertiti) changed her name from Ankhesenpaaten to Ankhesenamun. Thus both king and queen took steps to honor what came to be known as "the restored religion" of Amen.

As part of going back to the way that things used to be, Tut gave the priests of Amen their jobs back and let them receive money from the people of the land again. They used this money to maintain the temples of the gods.

The Egyptians built huge statues and temples to honor the different gods they worshipped, so under the advice of Ay and Horemheb, Tut helped to rebuild shrines (holy places) for many gods across the land, including in Luxor. His construction projects allowed the people to bring back many traditional festivals and religious activities that had disappeared during the time of his father.

Tut also restored capital buildings in the city of Thebes, moving the capital city back to that great city and leaving Amarna behind. Abandoned by all who lived there, the city quickly turned into a desolate and empty place.

After stabilizing things at home, Tut started rebuilding relations with nearby nations (especially the Syrian people of Mitanni) and oversaw wars with the nearby Nubians and peoples of Asia. As Chief of the Army, Horemheb went to Asia to personally fight in those wars. Some think that he was in the middle of one of those wars when young Tut died unexpectedly.

As Tut grew from a child king into a royal teenager, he felt more and more pressure to start a family with his older half-sister and wife. Ankhesenamun became pregnant twice, but sadly both of the babies died before they could be born. It seems like there had simply been too much incest in Tut's family. Because Tut's parents had been full brother and sister and because he was related to Ankhesenamun, Tut and his wife simply could not make a baby together.

As a result of the genetic problems he inherited from his parents and from the malaria he got from mosquitoes, Tut had pretty bad health through most of his life. Unfortunately, the situation got more complicated as the king got older. Walking got harder and harder, and his low immune system and frequent cases of malaria made him feel like he was sick more often than he was well. It was probably in the fall of the year 1323 BC when King Tutankhamen died.

We don't know exactly how he died, but there are some interesting theories that we will examine in the next section.

Although everyone knew that Tut had been sick most of his life, his death was still unexpected. Like most members of the royal family, he had been preparing a tomb in Amarna. But since the move back to Thebes he hadn't had the chance to start work on a new tomb. The nation had been so focused on Tut's construction projects (like the temple at Karnak) and on his economic strategies (like establishing new trade routes) that no one had thought that the young king would die after just 9 years or so of ruling.

So when King Tut stopped breathing at the young age of 18 or 19, it was quite a shock to his wife, his advisors, his people, and his allies. As was the custom, a group of priests got together and put the king's body through the long and complicated process of being turned into a mummy. The body was drained of fluids, the internal organs were removed, and it was finally wrapped in linens and put into a freshly-painted tomb...

...where it promptly caught on fire.

Chapter 4: What Happened After King Tut Died?

The people of Egypt had a very strong belief that that death was not really the end of anything but was in reality just a change to a different kind of life. They felt that a person who died really kept on living, just in a different place where they couldn't be seen anymore. The Egyptians also believed that a dead person could continue to make use of the things that they had owned during their life. It wasn't strange for important people (like pharaohs) to be buried with weapons, pets, or even servants – all of which were thought to go with them into the land of the dead.

So as soon as everyone realized that Tut had died, the clock began to tick. Tut was so young that he and his advisors hadn't yet prepared a burial place for himself. His possessions had to be gathered together, and his body had to go through a long process of being turned into a mummy. It seems that some the decorations of Tut's tomb (and maybe even the tomb itself) had originally meant for someone else – maybe Queen Nefertiti – and were quickly repurposed to serve as a resting place for the young king.

Unfortunately, such hurried preparations led to some errors while preparing Tut's body and tomb.

First off, the workmen assigned to prepare the tomb for Tut's burial were in such a hurry to finish decorating that the paint hadn't even dried before the chamber was sealed. Archaeologists who found the tomb years later saw traces of microbes that had grown on the wet paint.

But perhaps one of the most surprising finds was announced years after the tomb had been discovered. Researchers looking at small samples of Tut's bone and flesh found proof that his body had been cooked. This seemed strange, as preparing a Pharaoh's body for burial was a very sacred responsibility that the priests were very careful to carry out properly.

So how could a king's body get burnt after death?

After a lot of hard work and careful research, it seems like the oils used to preserve the body had been soaked up by the linen bandages that were wrapped around the king's body. After the body was placed into a series of three coffins, which were then put into a special room inside the sealed tomb, the temperature, humidity, and oxygen levels made for just the right conditions, and the oils on the linen began to smolder before eventually catching on fire.

Tut's body burned at nearly 400 degrees Fahrenheit while inside his sarcophagus.

Tut was buried in this golden sarcophagus[6]

The traces of fire that archeologists found were one of only several mysteries surrounding King Tut and his tomb. Another mystery (that still hasn't been completely solved) has to do with how the young king died.

Because he lived such a long time ago (and because very few official records from back then have survived to our day) no one can be completely certain how King Tut died. The only information that we have to go on is what we find in his tomb, including his body.

[6]   Image:
http://www.theslideprojector.com/art3/art3lecturepresentationssummer/art3lecture9.html

Because he had such poor health, some people who saw that his left leg had been broken shortly before death have assumed that this injury may have caused some sort of blood poisoning, which his sick body simply couldn't handle. Others saw a hole in the back of Tut's head and imagined a scenario where the young king had been murdered by someone who wanted his throne (someone like Ay). However, it was later learned that this hole had probably been made after Tut's death by Egyptian priests who had rushed the job of preparing his body for burial.

So is there any way to know how Tut died? One very recent explanation seems to make sense and to fit in with the available evidence. According to this theory, the young king died in a tragic chariot accident.

Dr. Chris Naunton from the Egypt Exploration Society compared Tut's injuries (including a crushed rib cage and pelvis) to injuries that victims of modern-day car crashes have. What did he learn? Dr. Naunton found that car crash victims and have virtually identical injuries as Tut, which makes him think that Tut must have been in a defensive kneeling position when he had some sort of a chariot accident – involving either his own chariot crashing or being hit by an oncoming chariot.

While the scene may seem strange – a king dying in a chariot accident – that is one of the most current theories and it seems to explain Tut's injuries. It might also explain why Tut's heart was not preserved (as was the normal tradition with pharaohs). If he was crushed by a chariot, then his heart would have been crushed also and unable to be preserved by the priests preparing him for burial. However, as interesting as this theory is, future discoveries may shed more light on how the king died.

One thing seems sure, though: King Tut was probably not murdered, no matter what some people may believe.

After King Tut died and was buried, there was chaos in Egypt. Because the young king had not been able to have any children with his wife, there was no clear replacement for the throne. Egypt had lost their king and it wasn't clear who the new king would be! While it seems that Tut had possibly selected Horemheb to take the throne after him, Horemheb was fighting a war in Asia when Tut died and arrived too late to help solve Egypt's crisis.

Many years later, a letter found by archaeologists helps us to understand the panic that some Egyptians felt after Tut died. The letter was probably written by Tut's widow Ankhesenamun; in it she begs the King of the Hittites to send her one of his sons as a husband so that she won't have to marry one of her own servants.

This letter reveals a lot about life in the days and weeks after Tut died. For example, it shows how tense things were in the royal court after the king's death. It seems like Ankhesenamun was being pressured by someone to marry her so that Egypt could have a king. Because it was common for a man to marry a dead king's wife in order to claim the empty throne, Ankhesenamun wanted to get married to a fellow royal person as soon as she could to avoid being forced into marriage to someone who may or may not have what it takes to be a good king. But who was this mystery person putting so much pressure on Ankhesenamun?

All evidence points to the royal advisor and to Ankhesenamun's own grandfather- Grand Vizier Ay.

The chart below can help us to understand the politics and family pressures that were going on behind the scenes during the time of King Tut:

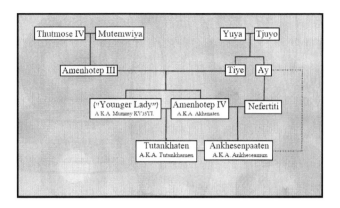

It is easy to understand why there was so much confusion after Tut died (and even easier to understand why his family was so sick), when we consider the facts in the above chart:

- Amenhotep IV married his full sister ("Younger Lady") and had a child with her (Tutankhaten).
- Tutankhaten married his half-sister (Ankhesenpaaten) but was unable to have children with her.
- Ankhesenpaaten later was pressured to marry her own grandfather (Ay)

The Hittite king who received Ankhesenamun's letter sent his son Zannanza to be her husband. But Zannanza never made it to Egypt, having been murdered on the way. Some historians think that Ay might even have murdered Zannanza so that no one else could sit on the throne that Ay wanted.

With no one else to marry, Ankhesenamun finally gave in to the pressure and married Ay, thus giving him the legal standing he needed to sit on Tut's throne. After conducting Tut's funeral, Ay celebrated his wedding and then became the new King of Egypt.

Horemheb was not happy with this turn of events.

Ay's reign did not last very long, mainly because he was an old man by the time he sat down on the throne. While it's hard to be sure exactly how long he was in power (for reasons that we will see in a moment) it seems that Ay was only king for anywhere from 4 to 9 years. But he used his time as king wisely.

With his kingly power, Ay continued the changes that he had started when he was advising Tut. He gave more authority to the priests and made a special temple in Medinet Habu that would later serve as his tomb. Not wanting Egypt to plunge into chaos again Ay made sure that he named a successor to the throne - a man who was probably his son named "Nakhtmin".

It seems that Ay wanted to start a new dynasty based on his family.

However, once Ay died after his short reign, Nakhtmin never sat down on his father's throne. Why not?

Because by that time Horemheb was back in town and he wanted the throne of Egypt for himself.

Horemheb wasted no time is establishing himself as the new pharaoh and as the final king of the 18th dynasty. Because he had always held such strong beliefs about how Egypt should be ruled (and because he wanted to punish what he saw as bad decisions by previous pharaohs) Horemheb went on a mission to disrespect all that Ay and Akhenaten had done. He replaced their names in historical records, he ruined carvings that were meant to honor them, and he did his best to make them disappear from history as if they had never existed in the first place.

Ay's cartouche (the symbol for his name) was almost completely erased from existence[7]

Unfortunately, this is something that new rulers do from time to time. Josef Stalin (Premier of the USSR) was famous for having members of his own staff murdered and then "erased" from photographs, as if they had never existed.

Josef Stalin made a man disappear from this photograph[8]

During his mission to disrespect the pharaohs Akhenaten and Ay, Horemheb was careful to leave Tut and his tomb in peace. While Horemheb did change the inscriptions on some of Tut's monuments and take credit for them, in reality he was probably the person who told Tut to do those things in the first place, so it may not have been stealing glory at all!

But Tut's tomb itself was left undisturbed by Horemheb - probably because Tut had shown him so

[7] Image: http://www.ancient-egypt.co.uk/petrie%20museum/pages/Petrie%20Museum%20(UCL)%20038.htm

[8] Image: http://www.disclose.tv/forum/a-brief-history-of-photo-fakery-t59931.html

much respect and had even made plans for him to inherit the throne.

After taking care of his personal grudges, Horemheb made changes to the politics of Egypt - further undoing what Tut's father Akhenaten had done. He gave power back to religious authorities across the country, established judges and courts, and worked on many construction projects.

Even though Horemheb took power away from Akhenaten's friends and returned it to the priests, he was still worried that the Amen priesthood might get too powerful and become corrupt. So he came up with what he thought would be a good solution: choosing the priests himself. Horemheb made some former soldiers that he had commanded into priests, mainly because he knew that he could count on their loyalty.

Horemheb's time as Pharaoh lasted for about 14 years, until his death. He and his wife had no children, and there were no more members of Tut's family around who could claim the throne. So Horemheb made arrangements for his Grand Vizier (special advisor) to take his place as king when he died. And that's exactly what happened.

Horemheb's vizier was named Paramesse, but upon becoming king Paramesse changed his name to Ramses I, thus ending one dynasty and beginning a new one. From now on, instead of the king's coming from Tut's family, they would come from the family of Paramesse (Ramses I).

With Horemheb's death, the 18th dynasty of Egyptian kings ended and the 19th began. Egypt would eventually be ruled by a total of 31 dynasties until being conquered by the Greeks in 305 BCE.

Today, of course, there are no more pharaohs in Egypt. The country has seen a lot of changes over the years, even as recently as 2011 when the Egyptian people rebelled against longtime dictator Hosni Mubarak.

The land of Egypt has changed a lot since King Tut was alive, but thanks to the preserved paintings, documents, and carvings in the tombs of kings like Tut we can still learn a lot about this fascinating time and people. In fact, the main reason that we know so much about Tut's time is thanks to the fact that his tomb was left pretty much undisturbed, and wasn't discovered until 1922, by British archeologist Howard Carter.

Howard Carter[9]

The entrance to Tut's tomb was buried beneath workers' huts for centuries, so grave robbers never got a good chance to break in and steal the valuable items inside. When Howard Carter and his team put together a series of clues to finally discover the steps leading into the tomb, it caused quite a stir. In fact, newspapers from across the world flocked to the Valley of the Kings in Egypt to cover the story.

On the day he entered the tomb, Carter chiseled open a corner of the door and peeked inside, letting his eyes adjust to the low light. As he smelled the ancient perfumed air wafting out of through the hole he had made, he saw his candle's light glinting off of

[9] Image: http://en.wikipedia.org/wiki/Howard_Carter

many gold and ivory treasures. Over his shoulder someone asked him if he could see anything. Carter simply said: "Yes, wonderful things."

Over a period of eight years, Carter and his team took pictures of, carefully examined, and eventually removed most of the items inside the tomb. The next to last section was the burial room, and it had four little structures built one inside the other. The innermost structure held the sarcophagus with the king's body.

Inside the tomb itself, there were objects of great value together with simple personal objects from Tut's life. There were canes used by the king to walk as he went about his daily duties; there were board games that he liked to play as a child; there was even a carved statue of the king's head and the golden throne that he used to sit on.

Most of the objects went to England to be displayed for the public, but others stayed in Cairo, Egypt, where tourists continue to visit them today.

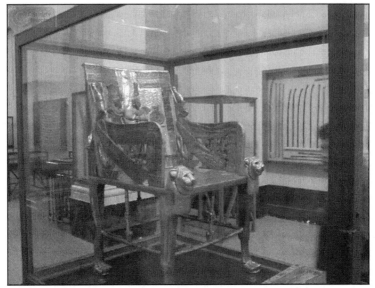
King Tut's throne as seen in a museum[10]

After discovering the tomb, Carter travelled to the United States to give lectures on what he had discovered, and in doing so he ignited the passions of the people he spoke with. He made them want to learn as much as they could about Egyptian culture and history.

In particular, people couldn't get enough of King Tut.

The world had finally discovered the boy king and had fallen in love with his story.

---

10 Image: http://www.stanouse.com/images%20Cairo/Cairo%20Sights/Pyramids%20and%20 Museums/pages/020%20King%20Tut's%20Throne.html

Chapter 5: Why Was King Tut Important?

King Tut and his tomb give us a window into life as it was in Egypt thousands of years ago. Because of people like Horemheb who destroyed historical documents and effectively erased the past, archeologists sometimes feel like they are trying to put together a puzzle with half of the pieces missing. But when Howard Carter found Tut's tomb and all of the treasures and objects inside, it was like finding an important piece of that puzzle.

King Tut's story showed us that Egyptian royal families of his time tried to protect their power by only marrying other family members, and we also learned of the scandals and intrigue that went on behind the scenes – like when Ay and Horemheb fought to take over the country after Tut died.

More than being just interesting reading or the stuff that makes for a good movie, the discovery of King Tut's tomb has helped the world to realize how important Egyptian history is. Even though we may have been born far away from Egypt and may have grown up in a completely different culture and spoken a different language, the modern world would be very different if not for the ancient Egyptians.

For example, if you brush your teeth in the morning, run a comb through your hair, and then lock the door to your house as you leave for school, you are benefitting from Egyptian inventions. If you learn geometry in school and run for P.E., you are doing the things that Egyptians made popular. And if you have a paper calendar hanging on your wall that divides months into four weeks and a year into 365 days, then you are using the same methods of keeping time that the Egyptians used.

When Pharaoh Khufu built his Great Pyramid in about 2560 BCE (more than a thousand years before Tut was born) he used the mathematics of geometry to measure the angles of the sides and the area of the structure. In fact, even though the huge tomb measures more than 750 feet on each side, no one side varies more than 2 inches from any other side. Their math was so precise that teams of workers building over many years could all follow the same plans and get a nearly perfect final result.

And because they closely studied the movements of the sun, the ancient Egyptians were able to notice cycles in the movements of the Earth around the Sun and the fact that these cycles were repeated every 365 days. So they decided to measure time based on these cycles, dividing the year into twelve months and each month into four weeks. They kept track of many of their discoveries, writings, and even commercial transactions on a new invention made from papyrus plants –something we know as paper.

Because of the well-preserved tomb of King Tut (and other tombs like his) we have been able to learn so much about the culture and discoveries of this ancient civilization. While it's true that we only get to see some of the possessions of the rich mummies (and not the common people), we can appreciate more about how the world that we live in came to be.

Tut and others like him help us to see that past generations were – in many ways – just like us. People fell in love, tried to make the right decisions with the information they had, and tried to make a better life for their children. King Tut died more than 3,300 years ago, yet through his tomb and the objects that were buried with him he speaks to us today.

The question is: will we listen to what he has to say?

50930327R00031

Made in the USA
San Bernardino, CA
08 July 2017